KT-450-779

Beautiful BRITAIN

NEWLANDS VALLEY, CUMBRIA

Beautiful BRITAIN

A journey through the most evocative and enduring landscapes of the British Isles

Bath · New York · Singapore · Hong Kong · Cologne · Delhi · Melbourne

This edition published by Parragon in 2007
Parragon
Queen Street House
4 Queen Street
Bath BA1 1HE, UK

Copyright © Parragon Books Ltd 2003

All rights reserved. No part of this publication may be reproduced, stored in a retrieval system or transmitted in any form or by any means, electronic, mechanical, photocopying, recording or otherwise, without the prior permission of the copyright holder.

ISBN 978-1-4075-0592-3
Printed in China

ENGLAND

IRELAND

SCOTLAND

CONTENTS

WALES

INTRODUCING BEAUTIFUL BRITAIN

Few parts of the world enjoy a landscape as varied as that of the British Isles, or can boast as rich a history packed into so small an area. This book draws together the many faces of England, Ireland, Scotland and Wales in a celebration of the magnificent geographical and cultural wealth that is our heritage.

A chapter of the book is devoted to each of the major regions of the British Isles, and in every chapter we have tried to highlight the spectrum of elements that gives each region its individual character and particular beauty. This beauty reveals itself in many forms – in the gentle slope of a distant hill and the craggy peak of a granite mountain, in the placid waters of a meandering river and the rushing torrent of a waterfall, in the dizzying heights of a precipitous cliff and the mist-wreathed rocks of a lonely beach – but each has the ability to move the viewer with its timelessness and power.

These natural wonders cannot fail to enthral, but there is also enchantment to be found in scenes that reveal the action of human hands. The regular lines of a cultivated field or the peaceful sight of a flock of grazing sheep remind us of our fundamental relationship with the land. A Roman fortification or a Saxon village enrich our present with the historical perspective that they provide. The crumbling walls of a once-impregnable castle or the geometric precision of a half-timbered house speak volumes about the political struggle and cultural background that has shaped this part of the world. A circle of ancient standing stones or the gravity-defying towers of a massive cathedral are testaments to the spiritual quest that touches us all.

Whether a panorama contains man-made elements or not, our appreciation of its uniqueness and charm is deepened by some understanding of the forces – be they geological, ecological, political, historical or spiritual – that brought the scene into existence. Some of the places depicted in this book have borne witness to significant events in our history, and some knowledge of these historical moments may colour our emotional response to these places. For example, the image that Glen Coe presents is perhaps little changed by human presence, but an awareness of the tragic events that unfolded there some 300 years ago can nonetheless inform and enhance our perception of this Scottish valley today. Throughout this book, therefore, we have endeavoured not only to present images of beautiful Britain, but also to give something of the context in which they are set.

VIEW TOWARDS ROSEBERRY TOPPING, NORTH YORKSHIRE
Also known as Odin's Hill, Roseberry Topping has strong links with the Vikings. It is situated on the Cleveland Way National Trail.

AN ANCIENT INHERITANCE

Britain's geological history is exceptionally eventful, and it is no coincidence that many developments in the science of geology have been made by scholars drawing their evidence from the British landscape. Over millions of years, the land masses that make up these islands have come together, literally from different parts of the globe, and collided. The land has then been tilted, raising up the ancient rock in the north and west. Ice has covered the surface of much of Britain, and glaciers and rivers have eroded the rocks to leave the mountains and plains, hills and valleys, lakes and streams that we see today.

Broadly speaking, Ireland, Scotland, Wales, Devon and Cornwall, with their many upland areas, consist of old, hard rock, which they share with Scandinavia and Brittany. Much of southern and southeastern England, especially East Anglia, consists of low ground and younger, softer rock, in common with northwest France. This is seen in the rugged hills and granite mountains on the one hand and the low plains and rolling downlands on the other, but there is a whole spectrum of types, both within and between these extremes.

This varied terrain combines with the latitude of the British Isles and their location off the coast of the European

"Though we travel the world over to find the beautiful, we must carry it with us or we find it not"

RALPH WALDO EMERSON, FROM ESSAY XII, "ART" (1841)

continent to give us our climate, and to determine the natural vegetation of these islands, from the almost alpine habitats of some mountainous or windswept regions, through coniferous forests and heather-clad moors to deciduous woodlands, ferny heaths, mossy bogs and reed-lined marshes. To these very different landscapes, the seasons, in turn, bring their own evocative palettes of colour.

These many natural factors affect more than just the visible character of the regions. Human history, too, has been shaped by the stage on which it has been played, by the mineral wealth beneath the surface, by the fertility of the land, by the accessibility of the different regions and by transport routes, by the presence of rivers, lakes and natural harbours. All of these factors have influenced where people have chosen to settle, build, farm, mine, trade or come together in towns and cities over thousands of years.

PEOPLE POWER

In turn, we, the inhabitants of these islands, have done much to affect the landscape. Certainly there are still areas of wilderness in the British Isles, scenes that would have looked little different 5,000 years ago, but they are few and far between. Our impact is seen most forcefully in the vegetation itself. For example, the clearance of the forests that once covered the chalk downs of southern England began several thousand years ago during the Neolithic period, and this process has continued over the ages. The rolling grasslands that we see today, therefore, are the result of grazing and cultivation, and the woodland that remains has been planted, but the vistas that the Downs offer are nonetheless inspiring. The attractive Norfolk Broads, too, are a man-made creation. The network of waterways that makes up the Broads was created by medieval peat cutters whose excavations have filled with water, but this unique and visually stunning environment is now one of Britain's prime wetland sites, supporting a flourishing range of plants and wildlife.

Fortunately, considerable effort, resources and good intentions are now being directed towards guarding these valuable habitats, and a significant number of the scenes that we have chosen for this book come from specially protected areas, including the National Parks, but it remains a fact that the great majority of the British rural landscape owes its appearance to largely human influences.

A SHARED HERITAGE

Many elements within the landscape of the British Isles echo the history of the peoples that have inhabited these lands. Some have battled to rule over the whole land, some have fought for independence, some have torn themselves apart in the search for self-definition, while most, throughout the centuries, have gone quietly about their business, making a living and raising their families. All, however, have contributed to the varied panoramas that Britain presents to the beholder, be it a megalithic monument or a steel bridge, a tilled field or a ruined castle, a remote mine or a towering cathedral.

It seems that it is only when you are showing the local highlights to visitors, be they from abroad or simply from another part of Britain, that you actually come to appreciate the full beauty of your surroundings. Creating this book has given us an opportunity to consider and present the diverse and historically rich landscapes of the British Isles. We hope that it brings you as much pleasure and pride in our natural and cultural heritage as it has brought us, and that it may inspire you to visit new parts of these precious islands.

WHARFEDALE, YORKSHIRE

The sheep have been taken in for the winter as wind-blown snow banks up against a traditional drystone wall high above the valley of the River Wharfe.

STEPPER POINT, CORNWALL

THE WEST COUNTRY

Few areas of Britain offer such a rich mosaic of landscapes as the southwest of England, from the hard, grey rock of Cornwall in the west to the soft, rolling chalk downs of Wiltshire in the east, from towering cliffs and sandy beaches to barren moorlands and richly wooded river valleys. Yet, despite this variety, the West Country has a distinctive character all of its own.

LONGLEAT MAZE, WILTSHIRE

THE WEST COUNTRY A GEOLOGICAL MOSAIC

At the southwestern tip of England, wind-driven rollers crash against the ancient granite rocks of Land's End, which look out westwards across the vast Atlantic towards the nearby Isles of Scilly and the Americas far beyond. Ocean currents carry the warm waters of the Gulf Stream all the way from Mexico to bathe the craggy coasts of Cornwall and Devon, bringing the early springs and balmy summers that make this a semi-tropical flower garden and a popular holiday destination. The seas also offer a rich harvest, and small fishing villages dot the coastline, their protected harbours bustling with colourful fishing vessels. Even the rocks hold their treasures, and the stone-walled shells of the pump houses of long-abandoned mines remind us of the tin and silver that once flowed from Cornwall along ancient trade routes.

This is a region steeped in myth and legend. The marriage of ancient Celtic tradition and Christianity can be seen in the ruins of Tintagel on the north coast, which popular belief associates with King Arthur. The once and future king is said to have defended this Celtic corner of Britain against the Saxons and he will one day return to save the country in its hour of need. Just off the the south coast of Cornwall stands the magical St Michael's Mount, which echoes its Breton cousin of Mont St Michel across the Channel.

Dartmoor, in south Devon, and Exmoor straddling the Somerset border in the north are wild uplands of peat bog and rocky tors, with a reputation for ghostly riders and spectral hounds. From their misty heights moorland streams flow down, swelling into broad rivers that reach the coast in picturesque wooded estuaries, offering a haven for the white-sailed pleasure craft of the holiday-makers.

To the east of Exmoor, we cross the Somerset Levels and Moors, with Glastonbury Tor rising in the southeast, thought by some to be the Avalon of old, King Arthur's final resting place and the site to which the Holy Grail was borne by Joseph of Arimethea. To the east, the land rises again, to the Mendip Hills through which the waters have carved the impressive Cheddar Gorge and the fairytale caves of Wookey Hole.

We come next to the rolling hills and vales of Salisbury Plain, the source of some of England's most beautiful chalk streams and evidence of the age-old human quest for spiritual expression, in the form of burial mounds and ancient henges, rings and avenues of gigantic standing stones whose meaning or purpose remain to be fathomed.

Turning south, we pass through the old market town of Shaftesbury as we head for the cliffs, beaches and sculpted forms of Dorset's remarkable coastline, a testament to the power of the sea. Directly to the south, across the English Channel and close to the French coast, lie the Channel Islands, of which Jersey and Guernsey are the largest. These islands have been British dependencies since 1066 when William the Conqueror, who as Duke of Normandy already ruled the islands, became King of England. As England's relations with France changed, the island was later fortified against the French, and further defensive construction took place under German occupation during World War II.

LAND'S END, CORNWALL

The most westerly point of the English mainland, 14km (9 miles) west of Penzance, Land's End is one of the country's most unforgettable landmarks. The huge granite cliffs that rise dramatically from the Atlantic Ocean and the romantic tales that adorn this location draw thousands of visitors every year. According to legend, the fabulous Lost Land of Lyonesse lies between Land's End and the Isles of Scilly, on the southwest horizon.

"Break, break, break,
On thy cold grey stones, O Sea!"

ALFRED, LORD TENNYSON, FROM HIS POEM "BREAK, BREAK, BREAK" (1843)

ISLES OF SCILLY

There are over a hundred of these very small yet beautiful islands some 45km (28 miles) off the southwest tip of Cornwall, and only five are inhabited. The remainder are home only to the seabirds. The climate here is so mild that the islands are said to have just two seasons – spring and summer. Flower growing is the Scillys' main source of income, and spring blooms can be picked as early as November in these sub-tropical conditions.

TINTAGEL CASTLE, CORNWALL

It was here at Tintagel, so legend has it, that King Uther Pendragon seduced the beautiful Igerna after disguising himself as her husband, Gorlois, Earl of Cornwall, with the help of the wizard Merlin. Arthur was born here as the result of that union. The castle that now occupies this rocky headland, however, was built in the 12th century for Reginald of Cornwall, the illegitimate son of Henry I. The cavern below the castle is known as Merlin's Cave, and the wizard's ghost is said to haunt it still.

ST MICHAEL'S MOUNT, CORNWALL

Known as the "jewel in Cornwall's crown", St Michael's Mount can be reached by foot at low tide across a 450-m (500-yd) granite causeway. At high tide, the Mount becomes an island, accessible only by boat. Local legend claims that the island was built by the giant Cormoran, and the Mount itself is dedicated to St Michael, whose apparition appeared to Cornish fisherman in AD495.

"Or whether thou to our moist vows deny'd
Sleep'st by the fable of Bellerus old,
Where the great vision of the guarded Mount
Looks toward Namancos and Bayona's hold;
Look homeward Angel now, and melt with ruth.
And, O ye Dolphins, waft the hapless youth."

JOHN MILTON, FROM "*LYCIDAS*, A LAMENT FOR A DROWNED FRIEND" (1637)

DURGAN, CORNWALL
The isolated fishing village of Durgan stands on the estuary shore of the River Helford. This sheltered arm of the sea, with its muddy creeks, shingle banks and rocky shores, offers a wide range of habitats and is remarkably rich in marine life. Just inland, in a warm and sheltered valley, lie the gardens of Glendurgan, now owned by the National Trust, in which many tender and exotic plants thrive.

overleaf **BUDE, CORNWALL**
Now a popular holiday resort, Bude was once better known for its wreckers, who lured hapless ships onto the jagged rocks of the North Cornish coast in order to plunder their cargo. In the 50 years between 1824 and 1874, the crews and passengers of some 80 ships lost their lives in this way.

DARTMOOR PONIES, DEVON

Dartmoor is the largest tract of wilderness in the southern part of England. It is also the highest place in southern England – and one of the wettest. The hardy Dartmoor pony has been grazing here since at least the time of Awlfwold of Crediton, a Saxon Bishop who died in 1012. In later centuries, when tin mining was an important industry on Dartmoor, the ponies carried tin to the nearby towns. When mining ceased, most of the ponies were turned loose to roam free on the moors.

WISTMAN'S WOOD, DEVON

One of Britain's rare remaining upland oak woods, Wistman's Wood lies on the boulder-strewn slopes of Dartmoor. It is designated as a National Nature Reserve in recognition of the importance of its outstanding wildlife and the lichens that thrive here in the clean, humid air. The deep shadows and strange, twisted trees give the place a mysterious atmosphere, and tradition has it that a pack of black, fire-breathing hounds sets out from here to hunt on the moorlands.

"River Dart, River of Dart:
Every year thou claim'st a heart."

ACCORDING TO LOCAL LEGEND, THE RIVER DART CLAIMS A LIFE EVERY YEAR

KINGSWEAR, RIVER DART, DEVON

The River Dart, bringing water down from the heights of Dartmoor, is one of the most picturesque and unspoilt rivers in Britain. After widening to form a natural inland harbour, the Dart narrows again north of Kingswear. Here, thick woodlands clothe the river's steep banks, giving it much of its beauty and atmosphere. The area is best seen from the water, and boating is a popular pastime throughout the River Dart's gentle lower reaches.

CORNHAM BRAKE, NEAR SIMONSBATH, SOMERSET

Autumnal colours amplify the deep beauty of Cornham Brake, in Exmoor National Park. This is Lorna Doone country, as depicted in R D Blackmore's novel. Although the smallest of the National Parks, Exmoor has over 1,000km (600 miles) of footpaths, and visitors are likely to see wild red deer, Exmoor ponies and horned sheep grazing on the moorlands.

TARR STEPS, NEAR HAWKRIDGE, SOMERSET

The medieval "clapper" bridge, known as Tarr Steps, crosses the River Barle near Hawkridge in Exmoor National Park. Seventeen flat stones, the largest of which is 2.6m (8.5ft) long and 1.5m (5ft) wide, span the 17-m (55-ft) river. No binding materials have been used in the bridge's construction – the bridge is kept in place by the sheer weight of the stones.

THE SOMERSET LEVELS, SOMERSET

One of the most important wetland areas in Britain can be found at the heart of the county of Somerset. Home to a wide diversity of wildfowl and waterbirds, the Somerset Levels is one of the largest managed areas of wet grassland and fens in lowland Britain. Most of the area is just 7.5m (25ft) above sea level, and it is drained by a system of ditches and drains. Constant vigilance against flooding is necessary, especially during the winter months.

"A deep frightful chasm."

DANIEL DEFOE, WRITING ABOUT CHEDDAR GORGE (1727)

GLASTONBURY TOR, SOMERSET

A distant view of Glastonbury Tor, with the 14th-century tower of St Michael standing on the top. In ancient times, the sea extended further inland across the Somerset Levels and the Tor became an island during periods of flooding and high tides. According to Celtic mythology, the Tor was the shrine of Gwyn-ad-Nudd, God of the Underworld. Glastonbury is also often linked with the Isle of Avalon, final resting place of the legendary King Arthur.

right **CHEDDAR GORGE AND CLIFFS, SOMERSET**

Cheddar Gorge is an extraordinary natural phenomenon linking the Somerset Levels to the Mendip Hills. In places, the limestone cliffs are some 140m (450ft) high. Cheddar is also home to the world-famous Cheddar cheese, first made here in the 12th century, when it was aged in the nearby caves.

STONEHENGE, WILTSHIRE

Built more than 4,000 years ago on an [illegible] of [illegible] and burial, the concentric stone structure [illegible] Plain in an area rich in Neolithic and Bronze Age [illegible]. The earliest parts of Stonehenge consist of [illegible] the Preseli Mountains in southwest Wales. The [illegible], the Sarsen stones, were brought from the [illegible]. The axis of the central horseshoe of stones is [illegible] sunrise on Midsummer's Day, but whether [illegible] a temple or a gigantic calendar, we may [illegible]. Stonehenge is now a World Heritage Site.

GOLD HILL, SHAFTESBURY, DORSET

Shaftesbury is a picturesque hilltop town, complete with 18th-century houses and cobbled streets. Gold Hill, which has often been used as a setting for films and television commercials, drops 215m (700ft) down a steep descent from the town's main street towards the Blackmoor Vale.

THE VIEW FROM GOLDEN CAP, DORSET

Golden Cap is situated one and a half kilometres (one mile) west of Seatown in Dorset. At over 190m (625ft), it is the highest cliff on the south coast of England, and ramblers reaching its top are rewarded with this stunning view of the surrounding countryside. The cliff gets its name from the rich yellow sandstone that covers its summit.

"They persuaded me to keep on, and at last stranded me on the pebbles, exactly opposite the magnificent arch of Durdle-rock Door. Here I stood and contemplated with astonishment and pleasure this stupendous piece of Nature's work."

JOHN O'KEEFFE, GEORGIAN PLAYRIGHT, 1792

left **CHESIL BANK, DORSET**
Running parallel to the coast and enclosing the Fleet lagoon, an area of brackish water that is rich in birdlife, Chesil Bank is a clay spit on which the strong local currents have deposited stones from the beaches of Devon and Dorset. It is said that if a local angler is put ashore in the dark on this impressive 29-km (18-mile) ridge, he can tell precisely how far he is from Portland Bill by the size of the pebbles, as they increase in size steadily from west to east.

DURDLE DOOR, DORSET
Situated to the west of Lulworth Cove, this spectacular natural arch is known geologically as an eyelet. Over the centuries, the power of the sea's waves has eroded the weaker parts of the Purbeck limestone rock formation. Durdle Door can be reached by a pleasant cliff-top walk from Lulworth.

WIMBORNE MINSTER, DORSET

One of the prettiest market towns in Dorset, Wimborne Minster is situated on the banks and water meadows of the River Stour. The 12th-century Minster features an astronomical clock and a "Quarterjack" figure who marks the passage of every quarter of an hour by striking bells.

GOREY, JERSEY, CHANNEL ISLANDS

The harbour at Gorey is dominated by the [illegible] Mont Orgueil Castle. It was built in the 13th century to protect the islanders against the French after King John lost Normandy to France in 1204. Originally called Mount Gorey, the name Mont Orgueil (French for "Mount Pride") was given to it by the Duke of Clarence, brother of Henry V, who was impressed by the castle's unique position and superb defensive strength.

BODIAM CASTLE, EAST SUSSEX

THE SOUTHEAST AND EAST ANGLIA

If the southwest of England looks out towards the Atlantic the southeast looks to Europe, both historically and today. And if, geologically, Cornwall and Devon have hearts of granite, then the counties of the south and east, with their bedrock of chalk, are far softer in temperement.

BEACHY HEAD, EAST SUSSEX

THE SOUTHEAST AND EAST ANGLIA DOWNS AND BROADLANDS

We start our journey in Hampshire, in the unique surroundings of the New Forest, which has been protected as a medieval royal deer-hunting ground for the last 1,000 years, and where horses and cattle still roam the open moors and graze in the dappled woods.

In the north of Hampshire, the 200-year-old Basingstoke Canal, which once connected Basingstoke to the Wey Navigation beyond Woking, in Surrey, has been lovingly restored to its former glory and now offers an amenity for boaters, walkers, canoeists, anglers and naturalists.

The chalk that we have seen on Salisbury Plain is a defining feature of the southeast, extending along the south coast and across the north of Kent, and its erodable qualities are seen clearly in the crumbling teeth of the Needles, where a ridge of chalk that runs through the centre of the Isle of Wight extends out into the sea on the west. Much of the island is a designated Area of Outstanding Natural Beauty.

As we travel eastwards from Hampshire into Sussex, we find ourselves in the gentle, rolling landscape of the South Downs on the ancient way that winds 170km (106 miles) from Winchester to Eastbourne. Bronze Age burial mounds and Iron Age hill forts can be seen on either side, reminding us that we are following prehistoric droveways that date back some 5,000 years. As we pass beyond the Devil's Dyke and Ditchling Beacon to the north of Brighton, the Weald can be seen to the northeast, and Ashdown Forest is just visible as a softening of the land. We turn towards the sea and admire the sinuous curves of the Cuckmere before climbing again to the cliff tops and making our way to Beachy Head, the most easterly of the white cliffs known as the Seven Sisters.

Further east, we are in "1066 Country" where William the Conqueror and his army landed and, having defeated Harold at the Battle of Hastings, brought Norman rule to England. Next comes Romney Marsh, a flat area of low-lying fertile arable land and rich pasture, with a unique landscape. At one time, all this land was covered by the sea, and parts are still below sea level, but sea defences now protect it.

As we reach the southeastern tip of Kent, the chalk reappears in its most familiar form – as the white cliffs of Dover surmounted by the impressive castle, a symbol of island Britain and its efforts over the centuries to keep invaders out.

To the north and west, the Garden of England spreads out in a vast, rolling patchwork of fields and orchards. Fertile soils and a mild climate combine here to produce a wealth of fruit, grain and vegetables, as well as the hops used locally in the brewing of beer. This region, which has more than its fair share of fine castles, has a rich history to tell, having witnessed the arrival of the Romans, the Vikings and the Normans, as well as the battle-filled skies of World War II.

Crossing the Thames, we come to Essex, once the Kingdom of the East Saxons and still closer in its history to London and Kent than it is to the counties of East Anglia that lie to the north. This relatively flat and low-lying region has an abundance of estuaries and marshlands along its coast, and a bleak beauty in its wide and open horizons.

The landscapes of East Anglia, too, owe much to the waters that flow through them, as evidenced by a tranquil scene of Constable country of Suffolk and the reed-lined waters of the Norfolk Broadlands. The low, flat skylines and level coasts of East Anglia have their beauty, too, as we see in a view of the shallow waters off Blakeney in Norfolk.

THE NEW FOREST, HAMPSHIRE
The New Forest was created in 1079 by William the Conqueror as a royal hunting ground. It retains many of the rural practices conceded by the Crown in medieval times, principally the pasturing of ponies, cattle, pigs and donkeys in the open Forest by local inhabitants known as Commoners.

"Nowhere in England rise such oak-woods, their boughs rimed with the frostwork of lichens..."

JOHN WISE, *THE NEW FOREST. ITS HISTORY AND ITS SCENERY* (1895)

BASINGSTOKE CANAL, SURREY

Here on a quiet stretch of the Basingstoke Canal at Woking, Surrey, the trees are turning golden at the approach of autumn. The once derelict 18th-century canal has been largely restored (a rebuilt lock is visible in the distance) and it is now regarded as one of the most picturesque canals in Britain.

THE NEEDLES, ISLE OF WIGHT

The Needles is the name given to a spectacular series of chalk formations that jut out of the sea at the western point of the island. The Needles Lighthouse, perched on the end of the outermost rock, was manned until 1997.

SLINDON ESTATE, WEST SUSSEX

Once owned by the Archbishops of Canterbury, the Slindon Estate is now a National Trust property. It comprises some 1,400 hectares (3,500 acres) of unspoilt beech woods and farmland set on the southern slopes of the South Downs, a designated area of outstanding beauty. The South Downs Way, which runs from Winchester in Hampshire to Beachy Head in East Sussex, is a popular route for walkers, riders and cyclists.

"Our blunt, bow-headed, whale-backed Downs."

RUDYARD KIPLING, FROM HIS POEM *SUSSEX* (1902)

KINGLEY VALE, WEST SUSSEX

Containing one of the largest surviving yew forests in Britain, if not Europe, Kingley Vale is perched high in the Downs of West Sussex. The forest, which is a National Nature Reserve, is thought to be more than 500 years old, and where the pure yew forest blends with deciduous trees it supports an amazing variety of wildlife, including deer, fox and badger, resident and migratory birds, snakes and lizards and a wealth of butterflies during the summer months. Aromatic herbs and several species of orchid are also found here.

CUCKMERE HAVEN, EAST SUSSEX

After flowing southwards through rolling downlands, the Cuckmere reaches the English Channel between the white chalk cliffs of Seaford Head and the Seven Sisters. In 1846, its meandering course was straightened by the creation of a channel down the valley, cutting off the winding loops of the river and creating a rich salt marsh sanctuary for waterfowl.

ALFRISTON CLERGY HOUSE, WEST SUSSEX

Called the Clergy House because it was at one time owned by the Church, this timber-framed, thatched house was built in around 1350, probably for a wealthy farmer. It stands beside the parish church in the delightful Sussex village of Alfriston, close to the River Cuckmere.

"The world is divided into five parts, namely Europe, Asia, Africa, America and Romney Marsh."

RICHARD HARRIS BARHAM, IN "THE INGOLDSBY LEGENDS" (1840)

SHEEP ON ROMNEY MARSH, KENT

Once covered by sea at high tide, the Romney Marsh region has been gradually reclaimed since Roman times to provide fertile pastureland. The sheep that graze here have adapted to this bleak landscape by developing hooves that are resistant to foot rot and fleeces that remain healthy in wet conditions.

THE WHITE CLIFFS OF DOVER, KENT

Long a symbol of homecoming for travelling Britons, the cliffs at Dover became a national icon during World War II through the popular Vera Lynn song "There'll Be Blue Birds Over the White Cliffs of Dover". On a clear day, the shores of France can be spotted across the English Channel from the top of the cliffs.

CHERRY ORCHARDS, NEAR SITTINGBOURNE, KENT

Known as the "Garden of England", the Kentish countryside is famous for the fruit that grows here, including cherries, apples, plums, pears and many kinds of soft fruit, thanks to the mild climate and fertile soils. During April and May, the orchards provide a stunning display of blossom.

OAST HOUSES, SISSINGHURST, KENT
The conical-shaped oast house, used for drying hops, is a distinctive feature of the Kentish landscape. Hops have been grown in Kent since the 15th century and were a vital ingredient for the once thriving brewing industry. Until recently, whole families would come from London for the summer to work in the hop fields, bringing in the harvest.

right **THE BLACKWATER ESTUARY, ESSEX**
A Thames sailing barge makes its way up the estuary of the River Blackwater in Essex. Until the advent of a more complete road system, these boats were the major means of moving freight on the east coast. The Blackwater estuary is an important wildlife and nature conservation site, renowned for the scarce plant species and rare birds that thrive here.

"I associate my careless boyhood with all that lies on the banks of the Stour; those scenes made me a painter and I am grateful."

JOHN CONSTABLE, ENGLISH LANDSCAPE PAINTER (1776 - 1837)

FLATFORD MILL, SUFFOLK

Willy Lotts' cottage, seen from the River Stour, was the setting for John Constable's famous painting The Haywain. *The cottage dates from the early 17th century. The valley of the river Stour around Dedham and East Bergholt provided inspiration for many of Constable's paintings.*

HORSEY WIND PUMP, NORFOLK

In the 19th century, more than 200 wind pumps like this one at Horsey Staithe worked to drain the Norfolk Broads. The Broads are a series of shallow lakes originally formed by medieval peat diggings that have long since flooded and are now joined together by a series of cuts and dykes. This unique landscape is famous for its boating and fishing, and for the reeds that are harvested for use in roof thatching. Horsey Staithe is still used as a loading place for reeds cut from the marshes.

BLAKENEY POINT, NORFOLK

Moored boats rest on the sandy seabed at low tide in the estuary of the River Glaveney, sheltered by Blakeney Point. The mudflats and saltmarsh areas around the bleak north Norfolk coast support a wide range of vegetation and birdlife, and attract hosts of summer holiday makers.

DOVEDALE, PEAK DISTRICT NATIONAL PARK, DERBYSHIRE

THE MIDLANDS

The English Midlands refers to the vast centre of the country, stretching from Gloucestershire and Oxfordshire in the south to Derbyshire and Nottinghamshire in the north, and from Herefordshire and Worcestershire on the Welsh border to the edge of East Anglia in the east.

MINSTER LOVELL HALL, OXFORDSHIRE

THE MIDLANDS THE HEART OF ENGLAND

This region merits its title of the Heart of England in several senses. A plaque in Meriden, some ten kilometres (six miles) from Coventry, claims that the 500-year-old village cross marks the centre of England, irregular though the country's shape may be. In the Midlands, too, lies the source of England's rise to industrial supremacy in the 19th century, with the growth of such steel-making centres as Sheffield and Birmingham, founded on the mineral wealth of the region. The extensive coalfields, around which many of the region's major towns and cities grew up, have been mined since the 18th century, though there is little mining now.

Human history is writ large throughout the region, with many ancient towns and settlements, Roman roads and medieval bridges, castles and stately homes, but there is a great deal of open country. Indeed, the Midlands has examples of almost all that the English landscape has to offer, from hills and high peaks to forests, river valleys, fields and hedgerows that reflect the reorganisation of the countryside that took place under the Anglo-Saxons. The only feature that the Midlands has in limited measure is seaside, but what little there is consists of the remarkable 150km (100 miles) of Lincolnshire coastline that includes the great estuaries of the Humber and the Wash, with its rich saltmarshes.

We start our tour of the region on the River Thames at Henley, in Oxfordshire, before moving westwards to the Vale of White Horse, with its ancient chalk carving. Heading north we come to the charms of a Cotswold village. The buildings here are made from the distinctive Cotswold limestone, grey in the southwest of the area, turning to honey colour as one moves northeast towards Banbury. The waters of the Thames start their long journey here on the eastern flank of the Cotswolds, flowing down between the Lambourn Downs and the chalk of the Chiltern Hills.

From the Cotswolds we turn west, cross the River Severn, and head towards the Welsh border to visit the lovely valley of the River Wye, which rises in the distant mountains of Wales, and we then move north into Worcestershire to the rolling Malvern Hills, source of the famous mineral water.

No visit to the Midlands would be complete without including historic Stratford-upon-Avon, the birthplace of England's most renowned writer and a typical Warwickshire market town. To the northwest is Shropshire, a large county with remarkable scenery, lying between Birmingham and the Welsh border, and here we visit Ludlow, which the very English poet John Betjeman described as the loveliest town in England. Here, too, is Ironbridge – a symbol of the vision, invention and engineering skills that drove the Industrial Revolution in Britain.

The northernmost part of the Midlands is the Derbyshire Peak District, an area of high moorlands and rushing streams, popular with walkers and also with anglers, who come to such rivers as the Dove for the excellent grayling fishing. The Peak District National Park covers 1,440 sq km (555 sq miles) and takes in parts of six counties.

Travelling east from the Peak District, the land gradually drops away as we cross the border between Derbyshire and Nottinghamshire and come to Sherwood Forest. Historical evidence is hard to come by, but the forest is world famous as the legendary home of Robin Hood. It is said that Robin and his band of "merrie men" once hid from the Sheriff's soldiers in the hollow trunk of the mighty Major Oak that still stands here, one of the largest and oldest oak trees in England.

Continuing eastwards, we are soon in Lincolnshire. In the northern part of the county there are two lines of hills – the limestone Heath and the chalky Wolds – but it is to the southeast that we make our way, through the peat and silt landscape of the low-lying Fens to the coast south of Skegness. Here the Lincolnshire Marsh meets the sea at a coastline made up of sand-dunes and salt marshes, and we visit the rich natural habitat of Gibraltar Point.

HENLEY-ON-THAMES, OXFORDSHIRE

This fine 18th-century five-arched bridge spans the River Thames at Henley. The course of the river is almost completely straight at this point, and an annual rowing regatta has been held here since 1839. After 1851, when His Royal Highness Prince Albert gave the event his patronage, the annual regatta became known as the "Henley Royal Regatta".

THE WHITE HORSE, UFFINGTON, OXFORDSHIRE

Possibly up to 3,000 years old and measuring over 110m (370 ft) in length, the White Horse of Uffington is believed to be the oldest chalk hillside figure in Britain. For centuries, local people maintained that it represented the dragon killed by St George on nearby Dragon Hill, but it is now generally thought to symbolise a Celtic god, possibly Epona, protectress of horses, or it may have served as a tribal landmark.

CHARLBURY, OXFORDSHIRE

Lying to the north-east of the Cotswold Hills, in the beautiful valley of the River Evenlode, Charlbury's mellow stone cottages have all the charm of a typical Cotswold village. The village's name suggests that it originated as a fortified Saxon camp. The ancient church is traditionally associated with St Diuma, the first Bishop of Mercia, who died in AD658.

overleaf **THE MALVERN HILLS, WORCESTERSHIRE**

Deriving their name from the Celtic for "bare hill", the Malverns consist of a 14-km (9-mile) range of low, rounded summits that run north-south between the rolling Herefordshire countryside and the flood plain of the River Severn. The hills of Wales are visible to the west from the top of the 425-m (1,394-ft) summit of Worcestershire Beacon, and Worcester, Gloucester and the Cotswolds can also be seen.

THE WYE VALLEY, HEREFORDSHIRE

Between its source deep in the Welsh mountains and its meeting with the River Severn some 240km (150 miles) downstream, the River Wye winds its way through the unspoilt landscape and fertile farmlands of Herefordshire.

STRATFORD-UPON-AVON, WARWICKSHIRE

The birthplace of William Shakespeare (1564-1616), Stratford-upon-Avon can boast of many memorials to the Elizabethan playwright and poet. Shakespeare was baptised and buried at the Holy Trinity Church, seen here across the River Avon. His wife, Anne Hathaway, was buried beside him in 1623. A memorial to Shakespeare, quill pen in hand, is on display at the church, and he receives a new pen every year on his birthday, which falls on St George's Day, 23 April.

"Into my heart an air that kills from yon far country blows;
What are those blue remembered hills,
what farms, what spires are those?"

A E HOUSMAN, FROM "A SHROPSHIRE LAD" (1896)

left **READER'S HOUSE, LUDLOW, SHROPSHIRE**
Ludlow, located 37km (23 miles) south of Shrewsbury, has many architectural jewels, including the ruined Ludlow Castle and some fine Georgian houses. Reader's House is a half-timbered Tudor building with an impressive porch, dating from 1616.

IRONBRIDGE GORGE, SHROPSHIRE
Building a bridge across the River Severn to replace the overworked ferry was the brainchild of his father, but it was Abraham Darby III who planned and oversaw this feat of engineering. Cast in huge sections at nearby Coalbrookdale, the 30-m (100-ft) bridge was erected in just three months in 1779, and it stands today as a monument to the pioneers of the Industrial Revolution.

THE PEAK DISTRICT NATIONAL PARK

Situated between Sheffield and Manchester, the Peak District was Britain's first National Park, set up in 1951. Its southern White Peak area consists of rolling limestone hills but here, near Buxton in the Western Area of the Dark Peak, comprising parts of Derbyshire, Staffordshire and Cheshire, the terrain is hard gritstone rock and peat bog moorland.

STANAGE EDGE, PEAK DISTRICT, DERBYSHIRE

Stanage Edge is situated in the eastern part of the Dark Peak, above the valley of the River Derwent. The hard gritstone in this area has long been quarried for building materials and to make millstones, but demand declined rather suddenly, as these abandoned examples testify.

"In Sherwood lived stout Robin Hood,
An archer great, none greater."

"HEY JOLLY ROBIN", 17TH-CENTURY BALLAD

SHERWOOD FOREST, NOTTINGHAMSHIRE
Although much of the woodland has now been removed, Sherwood Forest once covered an area of some 500 sq km (200 sq miles) and extended to the walls of Nottingham. The legendary home of Robin Hood, the forest probably became a private royal hunting ground under William the Conqueror, and was used by English kings from Henry I to Richard III.

right **GIBRALTAR POINT, LINCOLNSHIRE**
The Gibraltar Point National Nature Reserve on the Lincolnshire coast consists of salt marsh and sand dunes that have built up as the sea has retreated. Recognised as a site of special scientific interest, this unspoilt stretch of coastline protects important communities of animals and plants, including the sea lavender seen here.

DERWENT WATER, CUMBRIA

THE NORTHWEST OF ENGLAND

If the northwest of England conjures up an image of mills, busy ports, and large industrial cities, then it's a very partial image. Lying between the Pennines and the Irish Sea, and stretching from the northeast tip of Wales to the Scottish border, this is a region of beautiful landscapes that has a character all of its own.

BLENCATHRA, CUMBRIA

NORTHWEST ENGLAND PLAINS, HILLS AND LAKELAND

Cheshire is in the south of this region, with its low plains and rolling hills, and we begin with a view of Beeston Castle. To the north are the populated and industrial centres of Merseyside and Greater Manchester, and beyond them we come to the spectacular Lancashire Hill Country, which embraces the western flanks of the Pennine Chain, the valley of the River Ribble and the rugged Forest of Bowland, a designated Area of Outstanding Natural Beauty situated on the Bowland Fells.

The Ribble rises in the high moors of the Yorkshire Dales National Park and flows down the delightful Ribble Valley through the centre of the Hill Country, reaching the coast at the genteel seaside town of Lytham St Anne's, a far cry from the sparkle and buzz of Blackpool, just along the coast. Lytham boasts peaceful parks, half-timbered buildings, a Victorian pier and a fine promenade beside the sandy beach.

To the north is the vast expanse of Morecambe Bay, enclosed between the dramatic scenery of the Bowland Fells and the southern tip of Cumbria. This area attracts huge numbers of birds to feed on the fertile inter-tidal sands, and birdwatching is a popular pastime here, but the quicksands and incoming tides, which can move across the almost flat sands faster than you can run, pose dangers for the unwary.

Some 100km (60 miles) away to the west of Morecambe Bay, in the Irish Sea, the Isle of Man sits midway between England, Scotland, Ireland and Wales. Geographically part of the British Isles and historically ruled successively by the Irish, Scandinavians, Scottish and English, the island now enjoys a high degree of independence and has its own Parliament – the Tynwald – as well as its own currency, stamps and native tongue. Blessed by a mild climate, unspoilt countryside and secluded beaches, the Isle of Man is a popular holiday destination with a fascinating history to discover.

Returning to the mainland, the Lake District begins to the north of Morecambe Bay. Felt by many to be the jewel in the crown of English landscapes, this area is England's most popular tourist destination outside London and it's easy to see why. With a geological history of volcanic activity, considerable glaciation and subsequent erosion by the melting ice, the area offers an endless and varied panorama of stunning scenery. Lakes and corries, peaks and moors, rivers and deep valleys are to be found in every direction, and vast areas of the Lake District National Park are accessible only by foot, attracting hardy walkers and protecting this largely unspoilt landscape from the ravages of the modern world. Even for the less energetic visitor, there is a wealth of vistas, lakeside strolls and gentle boat trips to be enjoyed.

Lake Windermere is the southernmost of the lakes and the largest lake in England. Beyond its northern tip, in the area of Rydal and Grasmere, we are in true Wordsworth country, where he lived and wrote, first at Dove Cottage and then at Rydal Mount. Wordsworth's younger sister, Dorothy, described White Moss Common at the north end of Rydal Water as "a place made for all kinds of beautiful works of art and nature... miniature mountains, alps above alps".

To the east lies the tranquil lake of Ullswater, and away to the west are Crummock Water and Derwent Water, fondly known as "the Queen of the English Lakes", into which flows the steep-sided glacial valley of Borrowdale. The delightful market town of Keswick is situated to the north, close to the ancient stone circle of Castlerigg and overlooked by the mighty peaks of Skiddaw and solitary Blencathra.

To the northeast, lying between the Lake District and the high ridge of the North Pennines, is the valley of the River Eden, flowing north towards Carlisle and the Solway Firth. In its upper valley, south of Kirkby Stephen, we visit the ancient ruins of Pendragon Castle. We are close to the source of the River Eden, but also to the head of Wensleydale, which leads eastwards into Yorkshire and the northeast of England.

BEESTON CASTLE, CHESHIRE

The ruins of Beeston Castle stand on the red sandstone of Beeston rock, with excellent views across the Cheshire Plain. Built in the 1220s by Ranulf, Earl of Chester, the castle passed to Henry III in 1237 and was used as a prison during his wars with Wales. During the English Civil War, the castle was held by Royalists who were finally forced to surrender, and the defences were then destroyed on the orders of Parliament.

LANCASHIRE HILL COUNTRY

The Lancashire Hill Country comprises every kind of terrain – moorlands sprinkled with streams and small lakes, rugged hillsides, reservoirs, and several canals, including Britain's longest. The 204-km (127-mile) Leeds and Liverpool Canal climbs to a height of 150 metres (488ft) above sea level to cross the Pennines, and it links the seaport of Liverpool with the Aire and Calder Navigation at Leeds, forming a through route between the Irish Sea and the North Sea. Altogether, the region offers every kind of recreation and invites walkers, horse riders, canoeists, anglers and just plain sightseers.

"St Anne's is a beautiful place."

KING GEORGE V

LYTHAM ST ANNE'S, LANCASHIRE

Until the late 19th century, Lytham St Anne's was just a small farming and fishing community. A group of businessmen, however, saw the potential of this glorious stretch of sandy Lancashire coastline and began to develop the area into an "upmarket Blackpool". A pretty seaside town soon emerged from the wilderness of sandy dunes. The Victorian pier became one of the town's central features, attracting vaudeville artists and orchestras to entertain the visiting tourists.

MORECAMBE BAY, LANCASHIRE

Second only to the Wash, Morecambe Bay is the largest bay in the United Kingdom. It consists of 310 sq km (120 sq miles) of inter-tidal sand and mudflats and is one of the most important bird reserves in England. It is home to some 170,000 wintering waders, and several species arrive in internationally significant numbers, including oystercatcher, dunlin, knot, curlew, redshank and turnstone.

"Quocunque Jeceris Stabit.
(Whichever way you throw, it will stand)."

THE MEANING OF THE THREE-LEGGED SYMBOL OF THE ISLE OF MAN

PORT ST MARY AND PORT ERIN, ISLE OF MAN
Located in the Irish Sea, the Isle of Man is a self-governing kingdom with its own Parliament, laws, traditions and culture. Over 40 per cent of the island is uninhabited, and there are vast areas of unspoilt countryside. Its 160-km (100-mile) coastline also has many charms – high cliffs, quiet coves, pretty fishing ports and uncrowded sandy beaches.

right **BLUEBELLS, PORT ERIN**
In May, the wooded glens of the Isle of Man are awash with a stunning display of bluebells. The island is fortunate in having large areas of rich natural habitats that support an abundance of fauna and flora, including many wild flowers.

RYDAL WATER, CUMBRIA

At just over a kilometre (three-quarters of a mile) in length, Rydal Water is one of the smaller lakes in this part of the world. Its connection with the poet Wordsworth, though, makes it one of the most visited. At the western end of the lake there are some steps that lead to "Wordsworth's Seat" – said to be the poet's favourite viewpoint. Close to the lake is Rydal Mount, the house in which Wordsworth lived from 1813 until his death in 1850.

GLENRIDDING, ULLSWATER, CUMBRIA

Ullswater is considered to be one of the most stunning stretches of water in the Lake District. Set against a backdrop of breathtaking mountain scenery and surrounded by a gently curving shoreline of green fields, woodlands and sheer rock faces, this beautiful lake has been the inspiration for many artists and writers, including Wordsworth.

CRUMMOCK WATER, CUMBRIA

Tranquil Crummock Water is located southwest of the Derwent Fells and under Grasmoor Fell. A small stream links the southern end of the lake to Lake Buttermere. At the northern end of the lake, this stream becomes the River Cocker, flowing to the sea at Cockermouth. Crummock Water is one of the quieter lakes, and its beauty can be experienced by taking a gentle boat trip or a scenic walk that encircles the lake.

BORROWDALE, CUMBRIA

A popular spot for hikers, Borrowdale is a steep-sided valley that runs 8km (5 miles) from Derwent Water to the village of Seathwaite. The myriad shades of green that colour the valley only enhance the romance of this beautiful location.

"... a dismal cirque of Druid stones, upon a forlorn moor."

JOHN KEATS, REFERRING TO CASTLERIGG IN HIS POEM *HYPERION* (1795 - 1821)

CASTLERIGG STONE CIRCLE, CUMBRIA

Looking out across Skiddaw, Helvellyn and Crag Hill, Castlerigg is one of the most beautifully located ancient stone circles in Britain. The circle, which dates from about 3000BC, is best visited at dawn or dusk to capture it at its very best.

SKIDDAW, CUMBRIA

At 931 metres (3,054ft), Skiddaw is one of the highest peaks in the Lake District. dominating the skyline over the pretty Lakeland town of Keswick. The view from the top of Skiddaw is stunning – taking in Keswick as well as far-reaching views of Derwentwater Lake to the south and Bassenthwaite Lake to the west – and makes the long climb to the summit well worth the considerable effort.

PENDRAGON CASTLE, CUMBRIA

Pendragon Castle is situated in the Mallerstang Valley, south of Kirkby Stephen and close to the Yorkshire border. Its setting is dramatic, with Wild Boar Fell looking down upon the castle and the River Eden flowing close by, and legend has it that this is where Uther Pendragon, father of King Arthur, died. In 1341, the Scots set fire to the castle and it was abandoned. It was rebuilt, but fire destroyed the building again in the mid 16th century. Lady Anne Clifford had the castle restored in 1643, but it finally fell into ruin after her death.

SYCAMORE GAP, NORTHUMBERLAND

THE NORTHEAST OF ENGLAND

The distinctive beauty of the northeast of England is reflected in the number of National Parks to be found here. Of the ten National Parks formed in the 1950s, three are in the northeast – the Yorkshire Dales, the North York Moors (encompassing the North Riding Forest Park) and the Northumberland National Park.

FEIZOR, RIBBLESDALE, YORKSHIRE

NORTH-WEST ENGLAND CUMBRIA AND THE LAKELANDS

Together the National Parks here constitute over 425,000 hectares (a staggering one million acres) of spectacular landscape, not including the portion of the Peak District National Park to the west of Sheffield that falls within Yorkshire. The northeast coastline, too, is awe-inspiring, stretching more than 300km (190 miles) from Spurn Head on the Humber to Berwick-upon-Tweed on the Scottish border.

Much of the National Park land is moorland – high, barren, windswept and somewhat prone to rain, but such descriptions fail to conjure up the majesty of the landscapes or the uplifting sense of space that these wide horizons engender.

The spine of the Pennines is in evidence throughout much of the western part of this region, with all but a few of the many streams and rivers flowing eastwards from northern England's central watershed and making their way to the east coast. In the Yorkshire Dales, most of the valleys, such as Wharfedale and Swaledale, run true to form. Ribblesdale is an exception, flowing south and then westwards down the Ribble Valley that bisects the Lancashire Hill Country.

Geological history, during which successive layers of limestone have been laid down and then lifted up and faulted by major movements of the earth, has given the Yorkshire Dales their characteristic broad-backed hills, deep wooded valleys and spectacular limestone outcrops. Being porous, the limestone has been eroded to produce extensive underground passages and huge caves decorated with stalactites and stalagmites. The water itself has tricks to play, disappearing from sight as a small stream to flow underground for a while and then re-emerge as a river. Due to the faulting of the rock, many of the watercourses in the Dales make dramatic plunges down sheer falls before maturing into broad, though often fast-flowing, rivers in lush meadow-lined valleys, such as the lovely Swaledale.

Our survey of the coast starts at the tip of the Spurn Peninsula, which guards the mouth of the Humber. Although the lighthouse here is no longer in use, Spurn Head is the home of the Humber Lifeboat Station and Britain's only permanently manned lifeboat. Seven crewmen and their families live in this isolated but remarkable location. Continuing up the coast, to the north of Bridlington and Scarborough we come to sandy Robin Hood's Bay, bounded by the rocky promontories of North Cheek and South Cheek.

The northeast corner of Yorkshire forms the North York Moors National Park, which has the most extensive unenclosed heather moorland in England. This landscape of heath and bog is dissected by countless dales, some farmed and divided up by drystone walls and hedges, some deep, narrow and wooded. The rich birdlife here includes the golden plover and the merlin, and curlews are found along the coast. We visit the northern rim of the Moors and the romantic ruined priory of Guisborough, directly to the north.

Rocky headlands alternate with sandy bays all the way up the North Yorkshire coast as far as the mouth of the river Tees, and the last of the cliffs is Huntcliff, which rises sheer from the boulder-strewn beach below.

Crossing the River Tees and its rushing waterfalls we are in County Durham, and continuing north we come to the mighty Cathedral of Durham, sharing a rocky peninsula with Durham Castle and towering above the picturesque valley of the River Wear. Following the river upstream brings us to the tranquil landscapes of Weardale.

The spectacular Hadrian's Wall is our next stop, high on the Northumberland moors where the fortified wall that once marked the northern border of the Roman Empire runs up hill and down dale from the Solway Firth towards the east coast at Newcastle. Just to the south of Newcastle, at Gateshead, we take in a modern contribution to the English landscape in the form of the giant metal Angel of the North, before continuing along the coast. The Northumberland Heritage Coast extends for 95km (60 miles) from Amble to Berwick Upon Tweed, and includes such beautiful views as the long sandy beach near Alnwick and Dunstanburgh Castle.

Turning inland, we end our tour of the northeast region among the rolling hills of the Cheviots. Scotland lies beyond.

RIBBLEHEAD, NORTH YORKSHIRE
Here in the west of the Yorkshire Dales National Park, virtually on the border with Cumbria, several small becks start their lives on the high moors before meeting up to form the Ribble. The river then flows southwards, down Ribblesdale, and into Lancashire. This is a popular spot for walkers, just a short distance from the Pennine Way.

LIMESTONE PAVEMENT, MALHAM, NORTH YORKSHIRE

On the high ground between Ribblesdale and Wharfedale lies the great limestone pavement above Malham Cove. Made up of limestone blocks called "clints" separated by water-eroded spaces called "grikes", this is typical of many parts of the Yorkshire Dales. The melting snow and rainwater percolate through the rock and flow out of the limestone at the bottom of the Cove to form Malham Tarn.

SWALEDALE, YORKSHIRE

The most northerly of the dales that make up the Yorkshire Dales National Park, Swaledale is also one of the most beautiful. The River Swale, England's fastest flowing river, winds its way through a valley criss-crossed by traditional dry stone walls and touched by a thousand shades of green. Above the steep wooded slopes lie bleak, heather-clad moors, suitable only for grazing the hardy sheep that make Swaledale an historically important wool-producing area.

SPURN HEAD, YORKSHIRE

Some 6km (3.5 miles) long and only 50m (160ft) wide in places, Spurn Peninsula is a sandy spit that juts out from the Yorkshire coast into the Humber estuary. A distinctive black and white lighthouse, unused since the 1980s, stands in splendid isolation at its tip. The sea defences, the remains of which are seen here, were built by the Victorians and are now much in need of renovation to prevent the North Sea waves from destroying this unique and fragile environment.

ROBIN HOOD'S BAY, EAST YORKSHIRE

Colourful stonewashed houses and steep cobbled streets make this one of the most picturesque towns on the English east coast. According to legend, Sherwood Forest's most infamous outlaw kept a boat here ready for a quick getaway. For more law-abiding citizens, fishing provided the main livelihood.

ROSEBERRY TOPPING, NEAR GUISBOROUGH, NORTH YORKSHIRE

The distinctive conical hill of Roseberry Topping stands proudly on the northern rim of the North York Moors, on the Cleveland Way National Trail. The explorer Captain Cook lived in this region and his father worked on a nearby farm.

GUISBOROUGH PRIORY, GUISBOROUGH, NORTH YORKSHIRE

The wealthy Augustinian Priory of St Mary, founded in 1119 by Robert De Brus, was burnt to the ground in 1289, and only the solitary ruins of the east end of the church remain. It is said that a ghostly monk still guards the priory's hidden treasure.

HUNTCLIFF, NORTH YORKSHIRE

Once the site of a Roman watchtower, built as a protection against Anglo-Saxon marauders, the majestic 110-m (365-ft) Huntcliff stands east of Saltburn-by-the-Sea. The fort was overrun by invaders in the 4th century and was abandoned, but earthworks from the site can still be found on top of the cliff.

"Half church of God, half castle 'gainst the Scot."

SIR WALTER SCOTT, REFERRING TO DURHAM CATHEDRAL (1771 - 1832)

LOW FORCE, COUNTY DURHAM
The lovely River Tees has its source high in the Pennines in Cumbria, but it flows through County Durham's finest countryside. Low Force is a series of sizeable waterfalls in Upper Teesdale, northwest of Middleton-in-Teesdale. High Force, the largest waterfall in England, is an hour's walk further upstream.

right **DURHAM CATHEDRAL, COUNTY DURHAM**
Durham's striking Norman cathedral occupies a commanding position on top of a rocky peninsula in a loop of the River Wear. Begun in 1093, the cathedral was completed in 1274 and became one of the most holy sites of the Saxons. It still houses the mortal remains of St Cuthbert, as well as those of the medieval chronicler and poet, the Venerable Bede.

WEARDALE, COUNTY DURHAM

At one time the centre of the world's lead-mining industry (the valleys in this region were known as the "lead dales"), Weardale runs from west to east across County Durham between remote high moorlands. It once made up the second largest hunting ground in England (after the New Forest in Hampshire), and was used exclusively by the Prince Bishops for their "Great Chases". The local people were obliged to provide hounds, food, drink and shelter for the hunters.

HADRIAN'S WALL, NORTHUMBERLAND

Running the width of England, Hadrian's Wall once marked the northern limits of Rome's British border and the northwest boundary of the Roman Empire. Work on the wall began in AD120 and, although abandoned by the Romans in AD383, much of it still remains as a lasting legacy to the Emperor Hadrian.

"Men worked beneath the surface in the dark. Now in the light, there is a celebration of this industry".

ANTONY GORMLEY, SCULPTOR, ON CONSTRUCTING THE ANGEL OF THE NORTH ON THE SITE OF A FORMER MINE (1998)

ANGEL OF THE NORTH, GATESHEAD

Standing 20m (65ft) high and with a wingspan of 54m (175ft), the Angel of the North greets visitors to Gateshead. Designed by Turner Prize-winning sculptor Antony Gormley, the open-armed figure is seen by an estimated 90,000 car drivers and train passengers every day. Gormley constructed the work on the site of a former colliery pit head bathhouse and sees it as a tribute to the northern mining tradition.

DUNES NEAR ALNMOUTH, NORTHUMBERLAND

The Northumberland Heritage Coast is justifiably famous for its wild beauty and unspoilt, golden beaches. This area supports a great diversity of habitats, plants and animals, especially such seabirds as cormorants, kittiwakes, oystercatchers, fulmars and guillemots. Grey seals can also be spotted from the shore.

overleaf **DUNSTANBURGH CASTLE, NORTHUMBERLAND**

The ruined castle at Dunstanburgh dominates a lonely stretch of Northumberland's rugged coastline. Built in the 14th century by Thomas, Earl of Lancaster, the castle was enlarged by John of Gaunt, Duke of Lancaster. During the Wars of the Roses, a series of battles fought between the Houses of York and Lancaster, the castle was severely damaged by Yorkists and it then fell into ruin.

DUNLUCE CASTLE, COUNTY ANTRIM

NORTHERN IRELAND

The Province of Northern Ireland was created after the partition of the island in 1921. Its six counties – Antrim, Armagh, Down, Fermanagh, Londonderry and Tyrone – are part of Ulster, one of Ireland's four ancient kingdoms. Reminders of the region's history are everywhere, from the earliest settlements, through sites of kings and saints, to religious buildings, follies and castles.

TRADITIONAL COTTAGE, COUNTY FERMANAGH

NORTHERN IRELAND MOORS, MOUNTAINS AND MONUMENTS

Many parts of Britain display an amazing variety of geology and landscapes, but this is particularly true in the case of Northern Ireland. The largely rural tranquility of this region belies the turbulence of its geological past, which has seen the collision of two of the earth's tectonic plates and subsequent volcanic activity, followed by considerable glaciation. Add to these the action of the sea on the north and east coasts, the mild, moist climate and the erosive influence of streams and rivers, and the result is a landscape exceptionally rich in areas of outstanding beauty.

The historical influence of nearby Scotland can be seen in the design of many castles, and even in the planning of some towns and cities, for the arrival of Scottish Protestants in the 1600s led to the creation of Plantation towns, such as Londonderry, which are built around a characteristic central diamond. The Protestant influx also led to the sectarian conflict that has scarred the region ever since.

Water is a key element in the Irish landscape, and in County Fermanagh the Upper and Lower Lough Erne form a major waterway that runs from Fermanagh in the southeast to Donegal Bay in the northwest. To the northeast, the serene lowlands of the Erne Basin rise gently to the Tyrone Uplands and on to the dramatic Sperrin Mountains that straddle the border with County Londonderry.

The north coast of Northern Ireland is spectacular, to say the least, with its precipitous cliffs and the unique basalt formations of the volcanic Causeway Coast. The River Bann reaches the Atlantic here, flowing from the catchment area of Lough Neagh which, with an area of 386 sq km (150 sq miles), is by far the largest body of freshwater in the British Isles.

The northeast corner of the island looks out across the North Channel towards Scotland and the Mull of Kintyre, just 21km (13 miles) away. Turning south, the visitor can follow a winding road along the coast with the beautiful Antrim Mountains on the right, home to the famous Glens of Antrim, forested valleys with rushing streams and waterfalls.

The renowned view from the high slopes above Belfast City includes the city itself and the expanse of Belfast Lough. Geologically, the Lough and the Lagan Valley to the southwest are part of the Southern Uplands Fault that runs across Scotland from Edinburgh to Stranraer and continues right across Ireland to the Atlantic on the Galway coast. To the south of this fault line lies County Down, with the Ard Peninsula to the east, enclosing the sheltered waters of Strangford Lough. At the southernmost tip of the country are the Mountains of Mourne, a unique landscape that is justly celebrated in the famous Irish folk song.

Throughout the country there are countless reminders of the earliest inhabitants, who came here from the British mainland before the land bridge disappeared, but perhaps the most noteworthy of these is to be found at Navan Fort in County Armagh. Northern Ireland is the home of the United Kingdom's deepest Christian roots, and the nearby city of Armagh has held a prime position for almost 4,000 years, firstly as the seat of kings and for the last 1,500 years as the country's religious centre, chosen by Saint Patrick and now the seat of both the Protestant and Catholic archbishops. The fertile land to the northeast of Armagh was settled by people from Worcestershire in the 17th century and it is still a rich fruit-growing area, known as the Orchard of Ireland.

LOWER LOUGH ERNE, COUNTY FERMANAGH

The sun sets over the calm waters of Lower Lough Erne, which lies at the western edge of Northern Ireland. At the foot of the lough, the Erne flows across the border to meet the sea in Donegal Bay. Monasteries were founded on several of the lough's many wooded islands during the Middle Ages, and the southern arm of the lough is ringed with castles dating from the 15th to the 17th centuries.

HILL SHEEP, COUNTY TYRONE

Tyrone, the largest county in Northern Ireland, is home to the beautiful Sperrin Mountains, which stretch for nearly 65km (40 miles). The windswept upper slopes comprise blanket bogs and heather moors, but in the foothills lie wooded valleys and plenty of good grazing. County Tyrone has few large towns, but the many hundreds of ancient standing stones testify to the importance of this area during the Stone Age and there is a wealth of Celtic remains.

MUSSENDEN TEMPLE, LONDONDERRY

Set in the grounds of now-derelict Downhill Castle, this unlikely Italian-style rotunda has crowned the headland near Castlerock on the north Londonderry coast, since 1785. Built by Frederick Augustus Hervey, Bishop of Derry and Fourth Earl of Bristol, in honour of his young cousin Mrs Frideswide Mussenden, the temple is now owned by the National Trust and is open to the public.

"He lived most happy and content,
Obeyed no law and paid no rent."

SAID OF FINN MCCOOL IN IRISH FOLKLORE

THE GIANT'S CAUSEWAY, COUNTY ANTRIM
Geologists tell us that this field of some 40,000 basalt columns was created by the cooling of a flow of volcanic rock, but such awesome geometry deserves more poetic origins. To the more romantically minded, it is the handiwork of the warrior giant Finn McCool, who built the causeway in order to visit his lady love on Staffa, in the Hebrides, and bring her back to his home here on the shore of County Antrim.

right **WATERFALL ON THE GLENARIFF RIVER, COUNTY ANTRIM**
With its majestic scenery and rushing, tumbling waterfalls, Glenariff is known as the Queen of Antrim's famous nine Glens. The spray-splashed sides of the Glenariff River's steep gorges are rich in mosses, liverworts and ferns, and the Glenariff Forest Park, through which this small but beautiful river runs, is a national nature reserve.

BELFAST CASTLE, COUNTY DOWN

From its commanding position on the slopes of Cave Hill, some 120m (400ft) above sea level, Belfast Castle offers a wonderful view of the city and of Belfast Lough, one of the finest natural harbours in the world. The castle was built in the Scottish Baronial style by the Third Marquis of Donegall, and was completed in 1870. It was presented to the City of Belfast in 1934 and now houses many attractions for the visitor, including shops, a tavern and a restaurant.

right **NAVAN FORT, COUNTY ARMAGH**

Navan Fort, believed to have been Emain Macha, the ancient capital of Ulster, is now a circular grassy mound on top of a low hill to the west of Armagh. Part of a complex of forts and earthworks, Navan was an important site in the late Middle Bronze Age, about 1150BC, and the wealth of artefacts that has been unearthed here suggests that it continued to have ritual significance for a further 1,000 years.

MOUNTAINS OF MOURNE, COUNTY DOWN

Although the highest of their peaks – Slieve Donard – is less than 850m (2,800ft) high, the Mountains of Mourne are among Ireland's most visited sites. Only small shrubs and grasses such as heather and bracken grow on the shallow peat soil of this upland area, which is distinctive for its dry stone walls built of the local rounded granite boulders.

"When we've got all we want, we're as quiet as can be,
Where the Mountains of Mourne sweep down to the sea."

FROM A POPULAR SONG BY PERCY FRENCH, WRITTEN IN 1896

PUFFIN ISLAND, FINIAN'S BAY, COUNTY KERRY

THE REPUBLIC OF IRELAND

The very name of Eire, by which the Republic of Ireland is also known, conjures up music, myth and magic, and the land itself does not disappoint. This is a country of lush and fertile fields, sparsely populated plains, spectacular hills and mountains, dramatic rocky coasts and long empty beaches… and a great deal of history.

KILMALKEDAR, DINGLE PENINSULA, COUNTY KERRY

THE REPUBLIC OF IRELAND COVES, CAIRNS AND CROSSES

The Republic occupies five-sixths of the island, extending from Ireland's most northerly point, in County Donegal, to the southern tip of County Cork, and from Wicklow on the Irish Sea to the westernmost headlands of Kerry, Galway and County Mayo on the Atlantic. It comprises the ancient provinces of Connaught, Leinster and Munster, as well as three counties of Ulster Province.

With a population of less than four million people, 40 per cent of whom live within 100km (60 miles) of the capital Dublin, this is not a crowded country, and the visitor can drive for miles and see hardly another soul. English is generally spoken throughout Ireland, although there are Gaelic-speaking areas on the west coast.

In terms of its geography, Ireland takes the form of a shallow bowl, with rolling plains in the interior and a series of ranges of hills and mountains separating the lowlands from the coast. The principal rivers that drain the lowlands are the Erne in the north and the Shannon in the centre of the country, each of which consists of a sequence of long lakes leading ultimately to the west coast. The Atlantic coast is deeply indented, with steep cliffs, and is strewn with small islands, whereas the Irish Sea coast is more gentle and more regular.

Ireland's climate is very much influenced by its island character, surrounded by ocean currents that moderate the temperature, giving cool summers and mild winters, and providing considerable rainfall. The epithet of "The Emerald Isle" is well deserved, and rich greens are the dominant colours in much of the landscape.

The archaeological heritage throughout the country is a rich one, and the Republic has many earthworks and stone-built remains from Neolithic times, the Bronze Age and the early Christian period, as well as early fortifications. The most famous is Newgrange in County Meath, and this is where we start our journey. Most of the county is made up of a limestone plain with rich soils that have sustained settlements for many thousands of years, and this 5,000-year-old passage-tomb is one of the finest in Europe. It was discovered by chance at the end of the 17th century and has now been extensively restored.

To the south, in County Wicklow, lies the granite mass of the Wicklow Mountains, cut through by glens and wooded valleys. It is here, on the flanks of Kippure, that the River Liffey rises before flowing in a huge northward arc to reach the sea at Dublin. This county's wonderful scenery has earnt it the title of the "Garden of Ireland".

Travelling inland, we come to the Rock of Cashel in Tipperary, Ireland's largest inland county and one that boasts every kind of landscape, from the Knockmealdowns and Galtee Mountains to the wide plain of the River Suir. The 344-km- (214-mile-) long River Shannon flows through Tipperary, and the largest of the Shannon's lakes, Lough Derg, forms part of the border between Tipperary and County Clare to the west.

County Kerry, or "The Kingdom" as it also known, is in the extreme southwest of Ireland. With its three mountainous peninsulas and a low northern plain reaching to the estuary of the Shannon, Kerry has every visual treat to offer, and we visit the cliffs and sandy bays of the Dingle Peninsula, the dramatic peatlands and the beautiful lakes of Killarney before heading north.

In the historic city of Limerick we pause to watch the majestic River Shannon at the point where it becomes tidal on its journey towards the Atlantic. To the north we are in County Clare, a geological wonder with its unique limestone plateau – the Burren – and the Cliffs of Moher that rise vertically from the pounding Atlantic rollers.

Our next stop is in "Yeats Country", looking down on the massive limestone skull of Ben Bulben in County Sligo. Yeats is buried within sight of Ben Bulben. Despite its relatively small size, Sligo has the range of diverse landscapes that we are by now becoming used to, and Ben Bulben offers a spectacular view across the county.

Our last views of Ireland are of County Donegal. Geologically, this land is a continuation of the Scottish Highlands, and this can be seen in the dramatic cliffs, the deeply indented coastline and the undulating horizons of this most northerly tip of Ireland.

NEWGRANGE, COUNTY MEATH

The mysterious megalithic passage tomb at Newgrange was constructed in about 3200BC and is one the most important burial chambers in Europe. The kidney-shaped mound is surrounded by 97 standing stones, many of which are decorated with spirals and other geometric patterns. Archaeologists have discovered that at the winter solstice, the sun's rays shine through the roof box above the passage entrance and along the 19-m (62-ft) passage to illuminate the burial chamber.

WICKLOW MOUNTAINS, COUNTY WICKLOW
The heather-clad Wicklow Mountains National Park covers an area of nearly 20,000 hectares (50,000 acres) and provides a sanctuary for a wide range of moorland birds and other wildlife, including red deer and otters. This rugged landscape once proved a secure hiding place for Irish rebels after the 1798 uprising against the British. The Military Road, built by the British in their effort to find the fugitives, runs through the heart of this still largely unpopulated wilderness.

right **THE ROCK OF CASHEL, COUNTY TIPPERARY**
The name Cashel comes from the Gaelic "caiseal", meaning fortress, and this rocky stronghold has long been a base of both royal and religious power. The Munster kings, who ruled much of southern Ireland, chose the Rock of Cashel as their seat of power in the 5th century. In 1101, the site was handed over to the Church and it became an important religious centre. The Rock fell to Oliver Cromwell's army in 1647 in a bloody siege that cost 3,000 lives, and it was finally abandoned as a place of worship in the 18th century. Several impressive buildings grace the Rock, including the beautiful Cormac's Chapel and the Hall of the Vicars' Choral.

LAKES OF KILLARNEY, COUNTY KERRY
Killarney National Park is justly famous for the three stunning lakes that lie within its environs – Upper Lake (seen here), Muckross Lake and Lough Leane. The magnificent, moody reflections of the mountain ranges that surround them have inspired many poets and painters.

"I will arise and go now, for always night and day
I hear lake water lapping with low sounds by the shore;
While I stand on the roadway, or on the pavements grey,
I hear it in the deep heart's core".

THE LAKE ISLE OF INNISFREE **BY WILLIAM BUTLER YEATS (1865–1939)**

PEAT BOG, COUNTY KERRY

Blanket bog, which typically occurs in areas of high annual rainfall, covers almost one million hectares (2.5 million acres) of Ireland. Such bogs, or peatlands, have formed over the last 4,000 years and are composed of waterlogged vegetation, including sedges, grasses, heathers and mosses. Peat from this bog, located between Glenbeigh and Killorglin in the Ring of Kerry, has been cut, dried and used as fuel.

TRALEE BAY, DINGLE PENINSULA, COUNTY KERRY

This long, sandy beach with its spectacular backdrop typifies the charm and intense beauty of the Dingle Peninsula. Just 16km (10 miles) wide and 64km (40 miles) long, the peninsula is also blessed with a wealth of antiquities, ranging from Iron Age forts and beehive huts to early Christian oratories and stone crosses. Much of the area is still Gaelic speaking, and many signposts are only in the old language.

RIVER SHANNON, LIMERICK CITY, COUNTY LIMERICK
The Shannon, the longest river in Britain or Ireland, flows majestically through the city of Limerick. In the 9th century, fleets of Viking boats sailed up this mighty river to plunder and terrorise the local inhabitants. In later years, these Norse conquerors founded the trading port of Limerick. The ancient Thomond Bridge (seen here) connects the city mainland to King's Island, the heart of the medieval city. Once known as Englishtown, this part of the city is dominated by the 13th century King John's Castle, with its five drum towers and double gatehouse.

right **O'BRIENS TOWER, CLIFFS OF MOHER, COUNTY CLARE**
Composed of black shale and sandstone, the Cliffs of Moher stretch more than 8km (5 miles) along the Irish coast and rise to a height of 200m (650ft). Thousands of puffins, guillemots and kittiwakes nest on the sheltered ledges of this dramatic cliff face. O'Brien's tower, a disused tea-room from the Victorian era, can be found at the northern end of the cliffs.

"Neither water enough to drown a man, nor a tree on which to hang him, nor soil enough to bury him."

EDWARD LUDLOW, A MEMBER OF CROMWELL'S ARMY, DESCRIBING THE BURREN IN 1651

POULNABRONE DOLMEN, THE BURREN, COUNTY CLARE
Although seemingly devoid of vegetation (the word "burren" comes from the Gaelic "An Bhoireann", meaning "rocky place"), this limestone plateau is a very important botanical environment, supporting both Mediterranean and alpine plants. Many of these plants, which include maidenhair fern, a mediterranean orchid, mountain aven, spring gentian, hoary rock-rose, bloody cranesbill and dark red helleborine, are found nowhere else in Ireland. The Poulnabrone Dolmen, one of several ancient sites on the Burren, is a well-preserved portal tomb, dating back to 2500BC. Excavations have revealed the remains of some 20 men and women and an infant.

right **BEN BULBEN, COUNTY SLIGO**
On a clear day, the counties of Mayo, Sligo and Donegal can all be seen from the 527-m (1,443-ft) table-top mountain of Ben Bulben. According to Irish legend, Finn McCool found rest on Ben Bulben's summit after his victorious battle with Diarmuid. Ireland's most famous poet W B Yeats (1865-1939) spent much of his life in Sligo, drawing his inspiration from the surrounding landscape. He is buried in Drumcliff Churchyard, within sight of Ben Bulben.

"Now that she's so far away
from her dear old hills of Donegal,
I wonder does she ever think of me at all."

FROM THE SONG "HER DEAR OLD DONEGAL" BY LARRY KIRWAN, 1991

left **DERRYVEAGH MOUNTAINS, COUNTY DONEGAL**
County Donegal forms the northwest tip of Ireland with the Atlantic Ocean on three sides. In the centre of the county the glaciated Derryveagh Mountains rise to several peaks of more than 610m (2,000ft), the highest being Mount Errigal, at 752m (2,467ft). To the east lies Glenveagh National Park, 14,000 hectares (35,000 acres) of hills, bogland, lakes and woods (Glenveagh means "the glen of the birches").

GWEEBARRA ESTUARY, COUNTY DONEGAL
The Gweebarra river is approximately 40km (25 miles) long and flows west from Lough Barra to the Atlantic Ocean at Gweebarra Bay, a Designated Area of Conservation and an area of quite exceptional beauty. The Bay is home to around 500 common seals, and the estuary itself is rich in both marine and freshwater life. Angling is a popular pastime here, with excellent salmon and seatrout fishing throughout the summer.

HILLS ABOVE MONIAIVE, DUMFRIES AND GALLOWAY

THE SCOTTISH LOWLANDS

Scotland occupies about one third of the British mainland, with a total coastline of about 10,000km (6,200 miles), and can be conveniently divided into two distinct regions – the Highlands and Islands in the north, and the Scottish Lowlands in the south.

LOWLAND MOOR, PERTHSHIRE

THE SCOTTISH LOWLANDS HILLS, PLAINS AND FORESTS

The division between the Highlands and the Lowlands can be seen in the differing history and culture of the north and the south, as well as in the language, with the Gaelic-speaking people now restricted largely to the Hebridean islands and northwest Scotland while Lallans (an English dialect influenced by French and Scandinavian) is spoken mainly in the Lowlands.

The cultural division, however, has an underlying geological basis that is clear in the landscape. Running across the country, from the Firth of Clyde in the west to the east coast of Aberdeenshire, is a major break in the crust of Scotland that distinguishes the Highlands from the Lowlands. These two land masses were once separate, and their collision has given the two areas their very different characters, pushing up a massive mountain range in the north and causing great rivers to flow southwards carrying vast quantities of sediment.

This dividing line is known as the Highland Boundary Fault. The area immediately to the south is the Midland Valley, with Glasgow in the west and Edinburgh in the east. Most of Scotland's industry and most of the population are to be found here. Between the Midland Valley and the English border are the fertile plains and rolling glaciated hills of the Southern Uplands. Together these make up the Lowlands, an area with a generally mild, though often wet, climate influenced by the Gulf Stream, with landscapes rich in small lochs, forests, streams and rivers, and with a varied and plentiful range of wildlife.

We start our tour in the southwest, in Dumfries and Galloway, a region of hilly moorland and forests with an unspoilt and largely unpopulated coastline that looks south across the Solway Firth towards Cumbria and west across the North Channel towards Northern Ireland.

In the south, the waters of Loch Ken flow down the river Dee and past the island on which stands the massive 14th-century tower of Threave Castle, besieged by James II in 1455.

To the west we find ourselves in the Galloway Forest Park, Britain's largest forest park covering an area of 760 sq km (290 sq miles). Known as the "highlands of the lowlands", the park boasts such peaks as Merrick, which reaches 843m (2,765ft) and forms a magnificent backdrop to Loch Trool.

The Southern Upland Way passes to the south of the Loch. This walker's path runs for 341km (212 miles) all the way from the cliffs of Portpatrick on the west coast to the North Sea coast at Cockburnspath in the Scottish Borders, taking in all the features of the Southern Uplands on the way – peaks and moors, valleys and forests.

In the central lowlands, north of the Southern Uplands Way, we visit the countryside close to Lamington, in South Lanarkshire, near to the source of the River Clyde whose waters will ultimately flow through Glasgow and into the Firth of Clyde on the west coast.

Some 70km (40 miles) before reaching the east coast, the path passes north of the Eildon Hills through Melrose, following the River Tweed. When Robert the Bruce died in 1329 and his body was buried at Dunfermline, his heart was removed and taken on the Crusades by Sir James, "the Black Douglas". At the request of Robert's son King David II, his heart was brought back to be buried here, at Melrose Abbey, where it lies now.

At Melrose, the eager walker has the chance to turn southeast on St Cuthbert's Way, which runs all the way to Lindisfarne in Northumberland and passes the romantic ruins of Dryburgh Abbey. Some 14km (9 miles) to the west, the Firth (meaning estuary) is spanned by the mighty Forth Railway Bridge, with its three massive cantilever towers.

Returning westwards and passing to the north of Glasgow, we visit Loch Lomond, the only large lake to cross the Highland Boundary Fault, which passes through the island of Inchmurrin at the loch's southern end.

THREAVE CASTLE, DUMFRIES AND GALLOWAY

Standing on an island in the middle of the River Dee, Threave Castle can only be reached by boat. The island may once have been the seat of Galloway's ancient rulers, but the present tower was built by Archibald the Grim, 3rd Earl of Douglas, who died here in 1400.

NEAR LAMINGTON, SOUTH LANARKSHIRE

Here in the central lowlands, several ranges of relatively low hills divide up the landscape, causing the burns and small rivers to flow in all directions. The nearby Clyde flows westwards, but just across the hills lies Tweeddale, whose waters reach the east coast at Berwick, in Northumberland.

RIVER TWEED, SCOTTISH BORDERS

The writer Sir Walter Scott (1771–1832) considered this to be the finest view in all of Scotland, gazing across the River Tweed to the Eildon Hills above Melrose. Whenever Scott rode between Abbotsford and Melrose he stopped here, and it is said that as his funeral cortège made its way to Dryburgh from his home at Abbotsford House, his horses pulled off the road here out of habit.

DRYBURGH ABBEY, SCOTTISH BORDERS

Founded by the White Canons of the Premonstratensian Order in 1150, Dryburgh Abbey occupies an idyllic setting close to the River Tweed. The abbey was badly damaged at the hands of the English in 1385, but was rebuilt and extended throughout the 1400s. The Reformation spelt the end of monastic life in 1560. It is fitting that Dryburgh Abbey should be the final resting place of writer Sir Walter Scott, set as it is in the Border countryside that so inspired his novels.

FORTH RAIL BRIDGE, FIRTH OF FORTH

Opened in 1890 to carry the North British Railway over the Firth of Forth, the bridge crosses the river between South Queensferry and North Queensferry, to the west of Edinburgh. One of the greatest engineering achievements of all time, its construction utilised some 55,000 tonnes of steel and eight million rivets, including, according to legend, one solid gold rivet.

overleaf **LOCH LOMOND, LOOKING NORTH**
Considered to be one of Scotland's jewels, Loch Lomond is the largest freshwater lake in the country, 37km (23 miles) long and 192m (630ft) deep in some parts. Some 30 small islands on the loch add to its beauty and historical interest. St Mirren is believed to have founded a monastery in the 6th century on Inchmurrin, the largest island, seen here in the foreground.

BEN NEVIS, FORT WILLIAM, THE HIGHLANDS

THE HIGHLANDS AND ISLANDS

The Highland Boundary Fault rises from the deep Atlantic, cutting through the Isle of Arran and the Clyde estuary, through Loch Lomond and across Scotland to the north of Stirling, Perth and Dundee, reaching the east coast south of Aberdeen. Stand almost anywhere on this line and look north, and in front of you stretch seemingly endless mountains.

RED DEER STAG, HIGHLAND

THE HIGHLANDS AND ISLANDS REMOTE AND WILD

The sandstone and granite ranges of the Scottish Highlands occupy two thirds of Scotland. Ben Nevis is Britain's highest peak, at 1,347m (4,418ft), but there are 284 peaks that reach to more than 900m (3,000ft), known as the Monroes, and 210 peaks between 762m and 914m (2,500–3,000ft) in height, known as the Corbetts.

This is spectacular and rugged country, with few roads, little public transport, no motorways and very few people. The vast majority of the land consists of uncultivated, often inaccessible, rocky slopes, peat bog and heather-clad moorland. The shoreline is no less dramatic, incised by deep, fjord-like sea lochs, especially on the west coast, and away to the west and the north lie hundreds of islands, some little more than chunks of rock, but more than 100 of them inhabited. These are the Inner and Outer Hebrides, the Orkneys and the Shetlands.

It may take some effort to experience the Highlands and Islands, but the effort is worthwhile. Landscapes and seascapes with such grandeur and solitude are found nowhere else in Britain, and the wildlife is extraordinary – red deer, wild goats, otters, highland cattle, grouse, even wildcats and boars, can be seen if you are patient and fortunate. Seals frequent the coastal waters and the sea lochs, while seatrout and the famous Scottish salmon attract game anglers from all over the world.

We begin our visit in the depths of winter on the shore of Loch Awe, one of the many long, narrow lochs that give the west of Scotland its special character. To the east, the long neck of Loch Lomond points northwards. As we have seen, Britain's largest lake has one foot in the Lowlands, but the majority of it is north of the Highland Boundary Fault, as the surrounding mountains forcefully testify. Together with the Trossachs to the east and Breadalbane to the north, these peaks once formed part of a single chain that included ranges that are now in the eastern USA and Scandinavia. This upland area suffered considerable erosion during the last ice age, and many glens radiate out from the rainswept plateau of Rannoch Moor. To the northeast is perhaps the most famous and historic glen of all – Glen Coe, bounded on its north side by the blade-like ridge of Aonach Eagach and on the south side by "The Three Sisters". Glen Nevis, with its forested flanks is to the north, in the lee of Ben Nevis and the peaks of the Lochaber range. To the east, beyond the Grampians and the Badenoch Mountains, are the Cairngorms. From the northern slopes of Cairn Gorm itself, the water flows down through Loch Morlich, in the Glenmore Forest Park, before joining the River Spey, one of the most important salmon fishing rivers in the north of Scotland.

Further north, beyond the Monadhliath Mountains, the Great Glen runs for almost 100km (60 miles) in a straight line from Fort William in the southwest to Inverness in the northeast, literally dividing the Highlands in two. This active geological fault is composed of a string of lochs, the most notorious being Loch Ness, which is 40km (24 miles) long, 1.6km (1 mile) wide, and up to 240m (750 ft) deep.

Culloden Moor, on which Charles Edward Stewart, the Young Pretender, was defeated by the Duke of Cumberland in 1746, is close to Inverness. From here he made his escape to the ragged west coast, with its sea lochs, peninsulas and scattered islands, eventually reaching the lovely Isle of Skye, aided by Flora MacDonald, and from there he was taken to France. His arduous and circuitous journey had taken him to several of the Hebridean Islands, including the Isle of Lewis with its rugged headlands, sea lochs and long, solitary sandy beaches.

Returning to the mainland, the northern tip of Scotland has more contemporary royal connections, as we visit the Castle of Mey, close to John O' Groats, once owned by HRH The Queen Mother and now open to the public.

Our final ports of call take us beyond the north coast of Scotland, across the often stormy Pentland Firth and Scapa Flow to the islands of Orkney to view the stark beauty of this far-flung outpost of the British Isles.

KILCHURN CASTLE, LOCH AWE, ARGYLL

Overlooked by magnificent Ben Cruachan, Kilchurn Castle is located on a spit of land on Loch Awe. Built by Colin Campbell of Glenorchy in the mid 16th century, the castle was later enlarged to include the first purpose-built barracks in Scotland. In 1760, lightning struck the castle, causing considerable damage, and it was abandoned soon afterwards.

LOCH LOMOND AND THE TROSSACHS

Situated at the centre of the Loch Lomond and Trossachs National Park, the majority of Loch Lomond is well and truly in the Highlands. The region has an amazingly diverse geography, which includes alpine habitats, and it consequently supports a wide range of species, including some unique fish populations in the loch itself.

"Oh, you'll take the high road and I'll take the low road,
And I'll be in Scotland afore ye,
But me and my true love will never meet again
On the bonnie, bonnie banks of Loch Lomond."

TRADITIONAL BALLAD, ATTRIBUTED TO A JACOBITE SOLDIER ON THE EVE OF HIS EXECUTION

"Sure, by Tummel and Loch Rannoch and Loch Aber I will go,
By heather tracks wi' heaven in their wiles."

FROM THE TRADITIONAL SCOTTISH SONG "TANGLE O' THE ISLES"

RANNOCH MOOR, GRAMPIAN MOUNTAINS

Located between Loch Lomond and Glen Coe at an altitude of 300m (1,000ft), the glaciated granite and peat bog plateau of Rannoch Moor can seem a desolate place, but its countless small lochs and islets, its heather and stunted trees, give it a unique beauty. This is the watershed of central Scotland, and from here the waters flow to both the east and west coasts.

"Oh, cruel was the snow that sweeps Glen Coe
And covers the grave o' Donald
Oh, cruel was the foe that raped Glen Coe
And murdered the house of MacDonald."

THE BALLAD OF GLEN COE

GLEN COE, HIGHLAND
The beauty and serenity of present-day Glen Coe belies its savage history. In 1692, the MacDonald clan, who had a long-standing feud with the Campbells, were late in signing an oath of allegiance to William III, and the Campbells were able to gain government backing for a treacherous plan. For 10 days, members of the Campbell militia enjoyed the MacDonalds' hospitality while secretly plotting their downfall, and on the morning of 13 February, the Campbells turned on their hosts, massacring 38 members of the clan, including women and children. The remaining MacDonalds fled to mountain hideaways, where many more perished in the wintry conditions.

right **GLEN NEVIS, HIGHLAND**
Glen Nevis is one of the best examples of a glaciated valley in Scotland and also one of the prettiest. From its source at the peak of Ben Nevis, the River Nevis flows down through this picturesque Highland glen on its way to the sea.

LOCH MORLICH, CAIRNGORMS, HIGHLAND
The imposing 1,215-m (3,986-ft) Cairn Lochan provides a picturesque backdrop to Loch Morlich. The Cairngorm mountains, of which Cairn Lochan is a part, form the highest landmass in Britain (only the solitary peak of Ben Nevis is higher). The wild beauty of the mountains attracts many hikers, but the rapidly changing weather conditions can prove dangerous, even in summer.

right **URQUHART CASTLE, LOCH NESS, HIGHLAND**
The ruined 16th-century Urquhart Castle is perched on the northwestern shore of Loch Ness. The lure of Loch Ness owes almost as much to the "Nessie" legend as to the beauty of its surroundings. Ever since St Columba first spotted the beast in the 6th century, monster-hunters from all over the world have flocked here for a sighting of the legendary creature.

"Carry the lad that's born to be King over the sea to Skye."

FROM THE TRADITIONAL SCOTTISH BALLAD "THE SKYE BOAT SONG"

BROADFORD BAY, ISLE OF SKYE

Now linked to the mainland via a bridge, Skye is the largest of the Inner Hebridean Islands. It also has one of the most romantic historical associations – that of Bonnie Prince Charlie and Flora MacDonald. After the defeat of the Jacobite army at the Battle of Culloden in 1746, a huge ransom was placed on the head of Bonnie Prince Charlie. Flora Macdonald helped the Prince to escape to Skye, where, according to popular legend, the two fell in love. Broadford Bay, located in the southeast of the island, has views across to the Applecross mountains on mainland Scotland.

left **THE OLD MAN OF STORR, ISLE OF SKYE**

The Trotternish Peninsula, which lies in the northeastern part of the Isle of Skye, is notable for its extraordinary geological features, the most famous of which are the Old Man of Storr and the Quiraing complex. Precariously balanced on a basalt plateau, the Old Man of Storr is a stunning monolith, some 49m (160ft) high.

CASTLE OF MEY, CAITHNESS

Built by the Earl of Caithness in the 16th century, the Castle of Mey is located on the northern coast of Scotland between Thurso and John O'Groats and has superb views across the Pentland Firth. The castle was bought by the late Queen Mother after her husband's death and was restored as a summer retreat. It is said to be haunted by the Green Lady, believed to have been the daughter of the 5th Earl. According to legend, the woman fell in love with a servant, much to the dismay of her father, who locked her in an attic room. Distraught with grief, the woman threw herself from the attic window, and her ghostly presence now roams the castle.

TRAIGH LUSKENTYRE, HARRIS, WESTERN ISLES

One of the string of islands that makes up the Outer Hebrides, Harris is famous for its natural beauty and rich wildife, as well as for the tweed cloth woven here and on neighbouring Lewis. Traigh Luskentyre, a large sandy bay on the northwestern coast of South Harris, is surrounded by high sandhills that offer shelter to countless seabirds.

RING OF BRODGAR, ORKNEY ISLANDS

The Orkneys, which lie off the northeast coast of Scotland, have a remarkable collection of prehistoric monuments. The Ring of Brodgar, which is on the island of Mainland, dates back to the Bronze Age. Although only 27 of the original 60 stones remain, there is enough evidence to show that this was indeed one of the most impressive stone circles ever built.

LLYN GWYNANT, SNOWDONIA NATIONAL PARK

WALES

The singular landscape of Wales is rich in mountains, forests and rivers, with a wild 1,200-km (750-mile) coastline of rugged headlands and long golden beaches. Of the ten national parks formed in England and Wales during the 1950s, three are in Wales, and between them they constitute one fifth of the area of the country.

FAN FRYNYCH, BRECON BEACONS

WALES MOUNTAINS, LAKES AND LEGENDS

The Cambrian Mountains form the spine of the country, running the length of Wales from the Brecon Beacons and Black Mountains in the south to Snowdonia in the northwest. The Celts that settled to the west of this mountain barrier were largely protected against successive waves of would-be invaders, from the Romans, who built a huge military base at Caerleon on the River Usk, to the Normans and the Plantagenets, and to this day there are parts of western Wales where the majority of people still speak Welsh, a tongue descended from the ancient Celtish language.

In the lower lands of South Wales, the legendary King Arthur led the Celts in their defence against the Saxons in the 6th century, but Norman lords were later able to establish strategic castles at Chepstow, close to the English border, at Cardiff beside the River Taff, and in Pembroke in the southwest. Under the leadership of Llewelyn the Great, the Welsh fought hard against their overlords, but by the late 13th century King Edward I had conquered Wales and established fortresses throughout the country, including those at Harlech and Caernarfon. In 1401, using the recently introduced cannon, Owain Glyndwyr led a Welsh rebellion that succeeded in taking Harlech Castle, but the rebellion ultimately failed.

The coronation of Henry Tudor, a descendant of Llewelyn the Great, as Henry VII did much to heal the divisions between Wales and England, and Acts of Parliament under Henry VIII finally unified the two countries. This turbulent history has given Wales a greater concentration of castles than any other country in Western Europe, and this legacy is now an integral part of the beauty of the Welsh landscape.

We start our tour in mid Wales in the Cambrian Mountains, on the heights of Plynlimon, from which three rivers start their lives. It is the River Wye, flowing southeastwards, that we shall follow. At the northeast corner of the Black Mountains, on the edge of the Brecon Beacons National Park, we stand on Hay Bluff and admire the view. The River Wye is now below us to our north, and it is heading for the English border. We continue southwards to the beautiful Abbey of Tintern and, finding ourselves in a deep wooded valley, we are once again beside the Wye – the river has returned to Welsh soil after winding its way through Hereford and Worcester. Here the river echoes the line of Offa's Dyke, the earthworks that defined and defended the western border of Mercia against the Welsh in the 8th century.

Heading west along the coast of Glamorgan, the strange rocks of Nash Point look out across the Bristol Channel towards the north coast of Devon. Further west still, we come to the southwest tip of Wales, at Marloes Sands, amid the splendour of the Pembrokeshire Coast National Park, whose shores are washed by the Atlantic.

Now we return to the Cambrian Mountains, this time to see the reservoir of Pen-y-Garreg high in the Elan valley, fed by the waters of the Afon Elan and feeding, in its turn, the water needs of the English Midlands.

To the northwest, across the peak of Geifas, we visit the plunging waters of the Mynach Falls, rushing down to the gorge of the Afon Rheidol, born among the same hills as the Severn and the Wye but heading in the opposite direction.

Just over 30km (20 miles) north we are in Snowdonia National Park, gazing at the slopes of Cader Idris. The Park, with its countless mountains, valleys, rivers, lakes and forests, covers more than 2,000 sq km (800 sq miles). The roads that cross the park are mainly set in the valleys that separate large areas of mountain, forest and moorland and, apart from a few very attractive villages (where Welsh is the principal language), there is hardly a sign of human presence in this truly wild landscape.

The famous and historic castle of Harlech, lies on the coast at Tramadoc Bay, and the Afon Dwyryd reaches the sea a few miles further on, in the northernmost part of Cardigan Bay. Before continuing northwards we follow the coast round to the west and travel the length of the Lleyn Peninsula to the tranquil bay of Porth Oer.

The Menai Bridge, linking the Isle of Anglesey to the mainland, is a remarkable piece of engineering, and at the southern end of the Menai Strait stands Caernarfon Castle, a symbol of military might and a reminder of the changed relationship between Wales and the English Crown.

VIEW FROM PUMLUMON FAWR, PLYNLIMON, CEREDIGION

Plynlimon, in the south of the Cambrian Mountains, is the source of three rivers – the Afon (River) Rheidol, which flows quickly to the west coast at Aberystwyth, the River Severn, which heads northeast into England and loops far to the north before returning southwards, and the River Wye.

BRECON BEACONS NATIONAL PARK, POWYS

This is the view from Hay Bluff, one of the highest points in the Brecon Beacons National Park, which covers 1,345 sq km (519 sq miles) and comprises four distinct mountain ranges – the Black Mountains in the east, Fforest Fawr, the Brecon Beacons and Black Mountain in the west.

"Ah! rest awhile and contemplate the scene.
These hoary pillars clasped by ivy round,
This hallowed floor by holy footsteps trod."

EDMUND GARDNER, FROM HIS POEM "WRITTEN IN TINTERN ABBEY" (1796)

TINTERN ABBEY

Standing beside the River Wye in southeast Wales, Tintern Abbey was originally founded by the Cistercian order in the 12th century. It housed some 400 monks and was the richest abbey in Wales until the dissolution of the monasteries by Henry VIII in 1536. The romantic beauty of the abbey and its surroundings were recognised in the 18th century, and Tintern has since inspired Turner and Wordsworth, among others.

NASH POINT, VALE OF GLAMORGAN

The coastline at Nash Point is quite unique and results from the upheaval of sediments once laid down in tropical seas and now standing high above sea level. Glacial erosion and the action of the sea have left a series of rock pavements and crumbling, fortress-like bluffs.

PEN-Y-GARREG RESERVOIR, ELAN VALLEY, POWYS
The Pen-y-Garreg dam, built in the 19th century to supply water to the city of Birmingham, was designed to blend in with its surroundings and is a fine example of Victorian engineering. The Elan Valley is also an important wildlife habitat, renowned for its birdlife, including the rare red kite.

right **MARLOES SANDS, PEMBROKESHIRE**
The superb beach of Marloes Sands is located within the spectacular Pembrokeshire Coast National Park. The Sands are a designated Site of Special Scientific Interest (SSSI) due to the unusual cliffs that line the beach, which contain a range of sedimentary rocks formed about 410 million years ago.

MYNACH FALLS, CEREDIGION

One of the most popular tourist sites in Wales, the Mynach Falls can be reached by means of the narrow-gauge Vale of Rheidol Railway that runs 19km (12 miles) from Aberystwyth to terminate here. The nearby Devil's Bridge is thought to date from the 12th century and was probably the handiwork of the Cistercian monks of Strata Florida Abbey.

CADER IDRIS, GWYNEDD

Standing in Snowdonia National Park, in northwest Wales, the great rock of Cader Idris rises to a height of 890m (2,900ft). In legend, the mountain is the home of the giant Idris or the seat of King Arthur's kingdom, and it is said that anyone who spends a night on the haunted heights of Cader Idris will awake as either a madman or a poet.

"March ye men of Harlech bold, Unfurl your banners in the field,
Be brave as were your sires of old, And like them never yield!
What tho' evry hill and dale, Echoes now with war's alarms,
Celtic hearts can never quail, When Cambria calls to arms."

FROM "MEN OF HARLECH", TRADITIONAL SONG, FIRST SUNG DURING THE WAR OF THE ROSES

left **AFON DWYRYD ESTUARY, GWYNEDD**
The Afon Dwyryd starts its life in a small, unnamed pool above Tanygrisiau, in the uplands to the west of Blaenau Ffestiniog in North Wales, an area of peat bogs and slate quarries. Flowing down to the Vale of Ffestiniog, it is joined by the rivers Cynfal and Prysor before flowing out into the sea at Traeth Bach (meaning "little beach") at the northern end of Cardigan Bay. Every year, good numbers of salmon and seatrout make their way upriver to spawn in the upper reaches.

HARLECH CASTLE, GWYNEDD
The 13th-century castle, built by Edward I, dominates the town of Harlech. Perched high on a crag, the castle has superb views of Tremadog Bay, Lleyn Peninsula and the peaks of Snowdonia. One of the most unusual features of the castle is a fortified staircase cut into the cliff to allow supplies to arrive by boat, although the sea has now receded and no longer reaches the cliff. Owain Glyndwr, who led a popular national uprising, took the castle in 1404 and made it his stronghold.

186

PORTH OER, GWYNEDD

Located on the Lleyn Peninsula in North Wales, Porth Oer is a small but pretty bay. It is also known as "Whistling Sands", as the sand in the bay is said to emit a whistling sound or squeaking noise when walked upon.

MENAI STRAITS, ANGLESEY
The peaks of the northern Snowdonia National Park rise majestically behind the Menai Bridge, which links the island of Anglesey with the northwest tip of the Welsh mainland. Built by Thomas Telford and opened in 1826, it was the largest bridge in Britain at the time and the first suspension bridge of this kind in the world. The central span of 115m (376ft) is suspended from two "pyramids" by gigantic chains.

CAERNARFON CASTLE, GWYNEDD

Built on the orders of Edward I between 1283 and 1327, Caernarfon Castle is sited at the southern end of the Menai Strait between North Wales and Anglesey. Edward intended the castle to be a seat of government and to serve as a symbol of his dominance over the conquered Welsh. His son, also called Edward, was born here in 1284, and in 1301 was invested as the first English Prince of Wales. From this time onwards, the monarch's eldest son has traditionally been bestowed with this title. The investiture of Charles, the present Prince of Wales, took place at Caernarfon in 1969.

INDEX

ACKNOWLEDGEMENTS

We would like to thank everyone who has contributed to this book including many of the people who not only contributed images but maintained an enthusiasm throughout its progress. We would like to express our special thanks to: *Department of Tourism and Leisure/Lily Productions(IOM)Ltd; Dumfries & Galloway Tourist Board; English Nature; Northern Ireland Tourist Board; Northwest Tourist Board; Wales Tourist Board Photo Library and West Oxfordshire Tourism* for allowing the use of their pictures for free. Every effort has been made to trace the copyright holders and we apologise in advance for any unintentional errors or omissions.

We would like to thank the following for their time and patience:
©Stuart Abraham: 37; ©John Bailey: 15; ©Belfast Visitor & Convention Bureau/Jill Jennings: 122; ©Bord Fáilte Tourist Board: 130; ©Causeway Coast and Glens Marketing Consortium: 120; ©Charles Tait Photography Ltd: 170-171; ©Clive Streeter: 23, 49, 51; ©Colin Prior: 158-159, 163, 164, 167; ©Cumbria Tourist Board: 91; ©Dae Sasistorn: 50; ©Digital Vision: 2, 4, 6, 8, 9, 20-21, 64-65, 66-67, 74, 76, 88-89, 92, 95, 96-97, 98, 100-101, 102, 104-105, 112-113, 144, 148, 160-161, 162, 166, back cover; ©Dorling Kindersley: Kim Sayer 13, 19, 85; Tim Booth 62; Rob Reichenfeld 67, 68, 69; Joe Cornish 128, 131, 132-133, 136, 138; ©Dumfries & Galloway Tourist Board: 142, 145; ©English Nature: Peter Wakely 46, 72, 73; ©E.R.J Davey: 25, 26, front cover; ©Mike Harvey/PPL: 47; ©Isle of Man Tourism: 82, 83; ©Jason Hawkes Library: 12, 30-31, 62, 123, 139, 140, 141, 149, 165; ©Mike Kipling: 103, 110; ©Michael MacGregor: 154; ©Molyneux Associates: 146-147; ©New Forest District Council: 41; ©Northern Ireland Tourist Board: 114, 116, 117, 118, 119, 121, 124-125; ©North West Tourist Board: 78-79; ©Photography by Colin Palmer - www.buyimage.co.uk-contact 01279 757917: 168-169; ©Graeme Peacock 2002: 106, 107, 108, 109, 111; ©Paul Prestige: 16-17, 27; ©Robert Harding Picture Library: Neale Clark 150-151; Roy Rainford 178; David Hunter 180; Simon Harris 185; ©Iain Sarjeant: 168; ©Skyscan Photolibrary: 77; B Evans 14, 17; London Aerial 53; K Dwyer 129; R West 152-153; ©Stockbyte: 126, 134, 135, 137; ©The Forestry Commission: 156; ©The National Trust Photographic Library: Derek Croucher 18, 29; Joe Cornish 19, 56-57; David Noton 24, 44-45; David Sellman 28, 40; Mike Williams 33; David Hall 38; John Darley 42; Nick Carter 43; Andrew Butler 48; Stephen Robson 52; John Miller 54, 55; ©UKLandscape: Will Stanton 32; Baxter Bradford 34; Roger Holman 35, 36; Keith Plant 58; R Knisely-Marpole 70; Alex Rosen 71, 179, 188; Stephen Thaw 80; Jon Sparks 81; G C Whitwham 84, 87; Hemant Jariwala 86; John Dominick 90; John Potter 99; Alan Simpson 172; Mike Wilde 188-189; ©Wales Tourist Board Photo Library: 174, 175, 176-177, 181, 182, 183; ©West Oxfordshire Tourism: SWH 60 ; David Sellman 63; ©Yorkshire Tourist Board: 94.